Contents

Kids Can Save the world - 4

Kids are Awesome - 5

Mission 1: Only flush your poops! - 7

Mission 2: Donate don't dump - 8

Mission 3: Don't be a drag bring a bag - 10

Mission 4: No meat Monday - 11

Mission 5: Borrow don't buy - 13

Mission 6: Bars over bottles - 15

Mission 7: Turn it off - 17

Mission 8: Bee a pal - 18

Mission 9: Don't be a drip - 20

Mission 10: Bamboo Brush - 21

Mission 11: Recharge - 23

Mission 12: Don't waste it - 24

Mission 13: Keep it cool - 26

Mission 14: Leave the car at home - 28

Mission 15: Don't lose your bottle - 30

Mission 16: Turn off the tap - 32

Mission 17: Turn your house green - 33

Mission 18: Wear it twice - 35

Mission 19: Turn it down - 36

Mission 20: Provide for nature - 37

Mission 21: Don't be rubbish - 39

Mission 22: Shower Power - 40

Mission 23: Flying is for Superman - 41

Mission 24: Recycle - 42

Mission 25: Buy Recycled - 43

Mission 26: Mess it up - 45

Mission 27: Super-Clean - 46

Mission 28: Tree-mendous - 47

Mission 29: Keep it & See - 49

Mission 30: Zero waste - 50

Mission 31: Grow your own - 53

Mission 32: Banish that draught - 55

Mission 33: Buy Second-Hand - 57

Mission 34: Build a Superhero Home - 59

Mission 35: Plant trees as you search - 61

Mission 36: Thank you fridge - 64

Mission 37: Recycle your electronics - 66

Mission 38: Super flush - 68

Mission 39: Green Fingered - 69

Mission 40: Plastic Free Picnics - 70

Mission 41: Support Green Heroes - 73

Mission 42: Tree-mendous 2 - 75

Mission 43: Fossil Fuel Free Day - 77

Mission 44: Upcycling - 79

Mission 45: Re-Useable - 80

Mission 46: Old-School - 83
Mission 47: Buy Ethical - 84
Mission 48: The 3Ps - 86
Mission 49: Speak Up - 87
Mission 50: Share this book - 88
Awesome Resources - 90

Kids Can Save the world

50 AWESOME WAYS TO BE A GREEN SUPERHERO

BY

CLINT HAMMERSTRIKE

Kids are Awesome

You only have to look around the internet to see that kids are awesome. Kids like Greta Thunberg are changing the world and telling the adults what needs to be done!

However, it is not only supercool Swedish environmental activists that can change the world………

You can be a Green Superhero and save the world by:

- **Reducing** how much stuff you use.
- **Recycling** the stuff you do use.
- **Re-use** things that can't be recycled.

In this book, you will discover 50 superhero missions that you can undertake to become a Green Superhero and help do your bit to protect the planet.

As you complete each mission, colour in the picture of the planet so that you know you are on-track to become a Green Superhero

Mission 1: Only flush your poops!

Yes, you read that right. For this mission we need you to stop flushing the toilet when you go for a wee!

Every time you flush the toilet, you are using lots of water to flush away your wee and poop!

If you only flush the toilet when you go for a poop you can save up to 9 gallons of water a day!

By flushing less, you save water and reduce the amount of energy needed to clean and treat the water that comes into your home!

Be a superhero: Only flush the toilet when you poo!

Mission 2: Donate don't dump.

Sometimes as we grow up, we get too big for some of the toys we once loved playing with.

Instead of throwing old toys in the bin why not give them to someone else who can enjoy them.

You could donate them to a charity shop who can re-sell them to raise money for charity. Another option is to give them to someone else who you think would enjoy playing with them.

Plastic toys that are thrown in the bin can be harmful to the environment finding their way into rivers and the oceans and harming marine animals like whales, puffins and turtles!

Why not go around your house today and see whether you have any toys that you haven't played with for awhile that you could donate or give away to someone else.

Be a superhero: Give your toys a second chance.

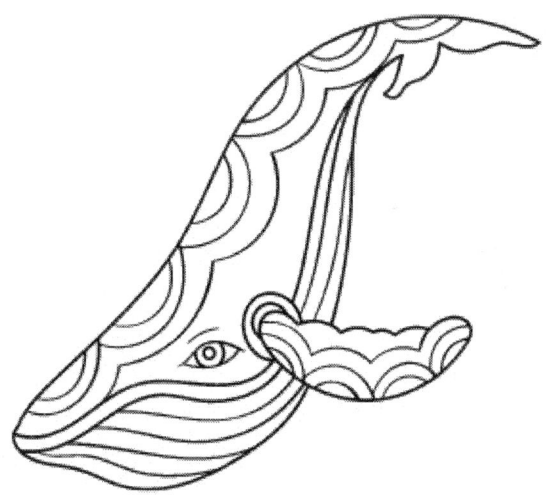

Mission 3: Don't be a drag bring a bag.

Single-Use Plastic bags are a supervillain and Superheroes hate them.

Next time you go to the shops, make sure you pack a re-useable bag like a cotton tote bag or a backpack. This way you can avoid buying unnecessary plastic.

Did you know that a plastic bag is used on average for only 12 minutes but take more than 500 years to break up when you dump them – releasing bad chemicals into the environment.

Be a superhero: Always bring a re-useable bag with you to the shops.

Mission 4: No meat Monday.

Could you and your family give up eating meat on Mondays! Why not find some tasty recipes online!

There are millions of people around the world who don't eat meat. They are called Vegetarians and choose not to eat meat as part of their diet. Often this because vegetarianism can be healthier, kinder to animals and have less impact on the environment.

By reducing the amount of meat you eat each day you can save lots of water and reduce the amount of trees that are cut down to provide land for grazing animals like cows.

Going veggie for the day is super easy, why not swap your regular sausages for a veggie sausage or eat a delicious veggie pizza instead of a pepperoni pizza.

Be a superhero: Make Monday a funday with a Superhero vegetarian dinner

Colour in and give this Superhero a cape

Mission 5: Borrow don't buy.

Every superhero knows it is better to borrow than to buy – except for pants!

Every time you buy something new (like a kite) lots of materials, water and energy is used in the making of the product.

By borrowing things, you don't need all the time instead of buying a new one; you are reducing the amount of waste you are responsible for.

A great example of borrowing is the library. By borrowing free books from the library instead of buying, you are saving loads of trees being chopped down for paper!

Are there things you could borrow instead of buying?

Be a superhero: Make the most of chances to borrow rather than buying.

COLOUR ME:

Mission 6: Bars over bottles.

The secret behind every great superhero……. super shiny hair!

The great news is you can now buy shampoo bars instead of in nasty plastic bottles. Available online and in shops everywhere, shampoo bars offer a plastic free hair-washing alternative.

Did you know that the number of shampoo bottles thrown away in the US every year could fill 1,164 football pitches! Imagine trying to play football on a pitch like that!

Remember, just by switching to plastic free alternatives you can save loads of plastic going to the dump and save lots of animals from plastic pollution.

Be a superhero: Switch from plastic bottles to plastic-free bars in the bathroom.

Colour the bottle in green when you have replaced your shampoo bottle with a shampoo bar

Mission 7: Turn it off.

A Superhero knows that leaving the light on when you leave the room is a big mistake.

Leaving the light on in a room we have left, wastes energy. Wasting energy is harmful for the planet and costs your family more money in electricity bills.

It is not just lightbulbs though. When you are finished watching TV, listening to the Radio or using a laptop you should always switch them off to save the most energy.

Did you know only 5% of the power drawn by a phone charger is actually used to charge the phone!

Be a superhero: Turn off lights and devices when you are not using them.

Mission 8: Bee a pal.

Insects like Bees are super important for our planet. They are superheroes sidekicks.

By planting bee friendly plants in a garden, allotment, balcony or windowsill you can provide an awesome food for insects like Bees.

The nectar of Bee friendly plants provides bees with energy to fly and nest, while the pollen provides bee grubs with the protein they need to grow.

Did you know that 1 out every 3 mouthful of food you eat depends on a pollinator like a Bee for its production.

Even though they are so important, the numbers of Bees across the world is in decline. This is because of destruction of their habitat and harmful chemicals are hurting them.

So let's give our superhero sidekicks a little help!

Be a superhero: Plant bee friendly plants wherever you can.

COLOUR ME:

Mission 9: Don't be a drip.

Wasting water is a big superhero no-no. Nothing hurts our ears more than the sound of a dripping tap!

Being water-wise in your house is a great way to protect the planet. Firstly, it takes a lot of energy to clean and deliver water to your home. Secondly, water is a precious resource and people (even superheroes) can't live without it.

Did you know a dripping tap could waste at least 5,500 litres of water a year? Enough to fill a paddling pool every week for the whole year.

Be a superhero: Get your parents to fix any dripping taps.

Mission 10: Bamboo Brush.

As well as keeping the planet clean, a superhero knows it is important to keep your mouth clean.

Lucky for you, you can do both of these at the same time. When it's time to get rid of your old toothbrush, why not swap from plastic to a bamboo toothbrush.

By switching from plastic to bamboo, you will be saving loads of unnecessary plastic going to the dump!

Did you know that it takes about 1000 years for a plastic toothbrush to decompose!

Be a superhero: Swap your plastic toothbrush for a bamboo one.

If you want to be a superhero always:

Mission 11: Recharge.

Why use something once then throw it when you can use it again and again and again.

Batteries power lots of devices, gadgets and toys. Lots of energy and chemicals go into making a battery so it's a shame to throw it away when it runs out.

To avoid throwing batteries away try rechargeable batteries. These can be re-used loads of times reducing air pollution, water pollution and climate change compared to disposable batteries.

Be a superhero: Go rechargeable over disposable for batteries.

Mission 12: Don't waste it.

Everyone knows a superhero is only as good as the food that fuels them.

So it's a shame when food is wasted. Roughly 33% of all food produced around the world is wasted and makes up a big chunk of gases that lead to climate change.

Did you know that an area larger than China is used to grow food that is never eaten every year?

As a Green superhero, it is important that we waste as little food as possible by only buying what we need and using up leftovers in tasty dinners.

If you need to dispose of food, why not try composting it if you have a garden or ask your local council for a free food waste bin. Food waste is collected regularly by the council and turned into compost, fertiliser and energy.

Be a superhero: Order a free food bin and don't waste food.

Mission 13: Keep it cool.

On a hot day, you can't beat a nice cool breeze. But we shouldn't be heating up the planet to cool down our room.

In many countries, the weather is so hot that air conditioning (AC) is needed to keep homes and offices cool enough for people to live and work.

The problem is that AC uses lots of energy that is bad for climate change. This is why should avoid AC where we can.

Instead of turning on the AC try closing curtains and blinds for windows in direct sunlight and opening windows in the shade to bring in a breeze that will cool you and your home down.

Best of all why not cool down by having a nice refreshing drink with ice cubes, or perhaps a yummy ice cream.

Be a superhero: Avoid using AC where possible to keep the planet cool.

Mission 14: Leave the car at home.

Think about all the super hero films. When do you ever seen a superhero travel by car?

By leaving the car at home and choosing to walk, cycle, scoot or take public transport like trains and buses we can keep fit, save money and help tackle air pollution and climate change.

Did you know that in the US cars and trucks make up 20% of all global warming pollution.

Air pollution from cars is also harmful to humans (and superheroes). Breathing in dirty fumes from cars is bad for our lungs and other parts of our bodies.

If you are going to be a Green Superhero, its time to get into training, so let's get fit and healthy and skip the car on short journeys!

Be a superhero: Leave the car at home and try alternative forms of transport.

Draw a superhero riding the bike:

Mission 15: Don't lose your bottle.

What do all superheroes need after saving the world? That's right a big drink of water.

But you won't see a Green Superhero using a throw away plastic bottle. Nope, a Green superhero knows that a bottle that you can use again and again and again is the super choice.

Did you know that since 1950 around 8.3 billion tons of plastic has been produced worldwide? That is the equivalent of 800,000 Eiffel Towers! What makes it even worse is that it takes more than 450 years for plastic to decompose.

Lucky for us there are many cool reusable bottles available that you can use every day to stop adding to plastic pollution and save money.

Be a superhero: Use a reusable drinks bottle and cut down on plastic pollution.

COLOUR ME GREEN WHEN YOU SWAP TO A REUSABLE BOTTLE:

Mission 16: Turn off the tap.

 When you are brushing, your teeth with your **Bamboo toothbrush** make sure you don't leave the tap on.

Turning off the tap between wetting your toothbrush and rinsing your mouth is one of the most effective ways to saving water.

Did you know that if you turn off the tap while brushing you could save 24 litres of water a day? That is a saving of one bath full of water every week!

Be a superhero: Turn off the tap while you brush your teeth.

Mission 17: Turn your house green.

Do you think Iron Man's HQ is powered by fossil fuels! NOPE. Superheroes always go green.

Every time you turn on a light, watch TV, charge a phone or laptop you are using electricity.

Regular electricity is created by burning dirty fossil fuels, which release harmful gases that are heating up our planet.

The good news is that you can easily switch from fossil fuels to renewable energy sources powering your home using the wind, sun and ocean waves.

Did you know that just one wind turbine can generate enough electricity to power 1,400 houses?

Switching to a 100% renewable energy provider is super easy to do online and can even save money.

Be a superhero: Get your house to switch over to a renewable energy provider.

WORD SEARCH:

W	B	I	O	M	A	S	S	J	T
I	J	S	O	L	A	R	H	E	I
N	D	N	O	P	W	S	C	Q	D
D	A	H	Y	D	R	O	B	U	A
G	E	O	T	H	E	R	M	A	L

WIND	GEOTHERMAL	TIDAL
HYDRO	BIOMASS	SOLAR

Mission 18: Wear it twice

Do you think superman washes his cape every day? Nope! Superman knows to wear it twice to save the planet.

Clothes like smelly pants and stinky socks need to be washed after you wear them. But other clothes like T-shirts, jumpers, skirts etc. don't always need washing.

By only washing our clothes when they need to be we are saving lots of water and stopping tiny bits of fabric being released into our environment - **NINE MILLION** plastic microfibers every wash!

Be a superhero: Only wash clothes when they need to be.

Mission 19: Turn it down

Most homes need heating during the winter. But making our homes too warm is heating up the planet.

In the UK 15% of the gases that cause climate change, come from heating homes.

By keeping our house slightly cooler (not cold), we can reduce climate change and save money. Did you know you can save £75 per year by turning the thermostat down by just 1°c?

And remember if you get chilly, there are loads of super simple ways to keep warm like putting on a jumper before you turn up the thermostat!

Be a superhero: Keep your house and the planet cool.

Mission 20: Provide for nature

A healthy planet is one where all sorts of wildlife have space to live, food to eat and fresh water to drink.

Whether you live the city or the countryside providing suitable food and fresh water is a great way to support a whole range of wildlife.

A simple option is to hang out a birdfeeder to provide food for birds. You can hang these in a garden, on a balcony or a window ledge depending on where you live. Why not check out the RSPB website for more information on how help look after birds.

Be a superhero: Put out food and water for birds or other wildlife.

Did you know?

1 in 2 turtles have eaten plastic

90% of seabirds have plastic in their stomach.

8 million tonnes of plastic our dumped in our oceans every year

Mission 21: Don't be rubbish

Nothing makes a super hero angrier than seeing litter. Only a supervillain doesn't put their rubbish in the bin.

Everyday objects that may seem safe to us, can be dangerous for animals – trapping, choking or being eaten by birds and animals. Putting our rubbish in the recycling/bin is an easy way to save animals from harm.

To be a real superhero, why not pick up and recycle/bin litter that you see. Always make sure you wash your hands well after touching rubbish.

Be a superhero: Keep your neighborhood litter free.

Mission 22: Shower Power

How do you think Spiderman washes after a busy day fighting crime? That's right, its shower time.

For a Green Superhero, the shower is a great option. The average bath uses 35 to 50 gallons of water, whereas a 10-minute shower with a low-flow showerhead only uses 25 gallons. **That's a lot of water saved!**

To go a step further why not try and keep your showers short to waste as little water as possible. Could you wash in less than two songs on the radio?

Be a superhero: Take a quick shower.

Mission 23: Flying is for Superman

Superman is lucky he can fly wherever he wants to go whenever he wants to.

Because we aren't Superman the only way to fly is to go by plane. The problem with this is that mile for mile flying is the worst way to travel for the climate.

Flying uses lots of fuel, which releases harmful gases into the air speeding up climate change. That is why a Green Superhero should try to use other types of transport that are less harmful like; trains, coaches or ferries.

Be a superhero: Try not to fly.

Mission 24: Recycle

Recycling is a superhero trick that allows us to use something until it's finished and then turn it into something else.

Recycling is the superhero way to make sure that nothing goes to waste. All kinds of things can be recycled and given a second life as something else.

Did you know that you can make a warm winter jackets from old plastic bottles? Or that egg boxes can be made from old newspapers!

Why not be a superhero and make sure your house is recycling as much as possible. Check out recyclenow.com for more information.

Be a superhero: Recycle your waste

Mission 25: Buy Recycled

A superhero knows that it is better to re-use something rather than make a new one.

By recycling we are able to extend the life of materials like plastic that otherwise would be dumped and cause harm to animals and our environment.

The superhero move is to buy things made from recycled material rather than new material.

Did you know that you can buy recycled sports clothes, shoes, Jenga, backpacks, dog collars, cups and much, much more?

Be a superhero: Buy recycled products where you can.

WORD SEARCH:

C	E	R	E	C	Y	C	L	E	Q
L	R	E	V	P	G	M	X	J	A
I	H	D	B	U	R	N	F	W	Y
M	K	U	Q	D	E	L	U	A	S
A	O	C	K	T	E	P	I	S	D
T	U	E	Z	U	N	F	T	T	F
E	B	G	A	R	E	U	S	E	V
X	M	O	U	N	T	A	I	N	O
O	C	E	A	N	B	N	H	I	P
W	A	Y	P	L	A	S	T	I	C

CLIMATE	REDUCE	WASTE
RECYCLE	PLASTIC	REUSE
OCEAN	MOUNTAIN	GREEN

Mission 26: Mess it up

While having a tidy garden, balcony or allotment looks nice it's not always great for nature.

Insects, birds and small animals don't love regularly cut lawns and overly tidy gardens. By letting lawns grow longer, you are making space for plants and insects including butterflies and wildflowers.

By only mowing the grass once a month, you give plants like daisies and white clover a chance to grow – which is great for bees.

Did you know leaving a gap at the bottom of your fence allows wildlife like hedgehogs to move around?

Be a superhero: Let your grass grown and create space for nature.

Mission 27: Super-Clean

Keeping your house clean is important. But cleaning your home shouldn't make the planet dirty.

Lots of cleaning supplies used in the home contain harmful chemicals that are bad for the environment and take a lot of energy to make.

By making your own cleaning supplies you can use sustainable and naturally safe and non-toxic ingredients that don't hurt the environment.

You can find loads of recipes for simple traditional cleaning supplies such as; surface cleaner, window spray, oven cleaner and much more. **Always make these with the help of an adult.**

Be a superhero: Make your own natural cleaning supplies

Mission 28: Tree-mendous

Did you know that the paper for this book came from a tree?

We rely on trees for making loads of useful things like paper, furniture, boats and much more.

However, trees are also super important for our environment. They provide us with oxygen to breathe, food to eat, keep our planet cool and provide homes for all sorts of wildlife.

That is why it is crucial that we don't cut down too many trees or waste things made from trees. One simple way to do this is to use technology to avoid having to print out things like tickets or other documents.

And of course as superheroes, we know that when we are buying paper we should always buy recycled paper.

Did you know that it takes 70% less energy and water to recycle paper than to create new paper? Best of all recycling one ton of paper (about the size of a small car) saves 17 trees being cut down.

Be a superhero: Use technology to avoid unnecessary printing and always buy recycled paper.

COLOUR ME:

Mission 29: Keep it & See

Do you know how much rubbish you and your family produce? I bet you it is more than you think.

Did you know that the average home in the UK produces more than a tonne of waste every year? This comes to a total of 31 million tonnes per year; this is the same weight as 3,500,000 double decker buses!

By reducing the amount of rubbish we throw away, we can help protect the environment. To get an idea of how much rubbish is thrown away write a rubbish journal of everything that is thrown in the bin.

Be a superhero: Keep a rubbish diary of everything you throw away.

Mission 30: Zero waste

So now you know how much rubbish you create. It's time to make an awesome plan to fight waste.

That plan is called "Zero Waste". By buying things without packaging, you can reduce the amount of waste you create. A great example of this is not using a plastic bag to put your fruit and veg in at the supermarket.

Where you have to buy things with packaging try and avoid non-recyclable plastic containers and opt for cardboard or glass packaging, which can be recycled or re-used.

Did you know that 40% of plastic produced is packaging used just once and then thrown away.

If you really want to cut down on waste, why not search online for your nearest zero-waste supermarket where you can buy everything from cereal to washing up liquid without any packaging. It's simple you bring your own re-usable bottles and containers and simply buy what you need.

Be a superhero: Buy zero-waste.

Going ZERO WASTE

=

Saves resources and reduces pollution

Helps reduce global warming

Preserves natural resources

Mission 31: Grow your own

A Green Superhero knows that nothing tastes better than food you have grown yourself!

Growing your own food is super simple. All you need is a pot, some soil and a few seeds. In a garden, balcony or windowsill it is possible to grow a whole range of delicious fruit, vegetables and herbs.

Because the majority of food sold in supermarkets goes through a long process of being picked, shipped and displayed in shops they lose their freshness and goodness. By growing food at home, you can pick when the food is ripest and be eating it in minutes.

Some easy foods to grow include: courgette, chili peppers, beans, potatoes, strawberries, salad leaves, basil, coriander, sage and chives.

So why not be a green-fingered Superhero and try and grow yourself some awesome fresh food

Be a superhero: Try growing some yummy fresh fruit, vegetables and herbs.

COLOUR ME:

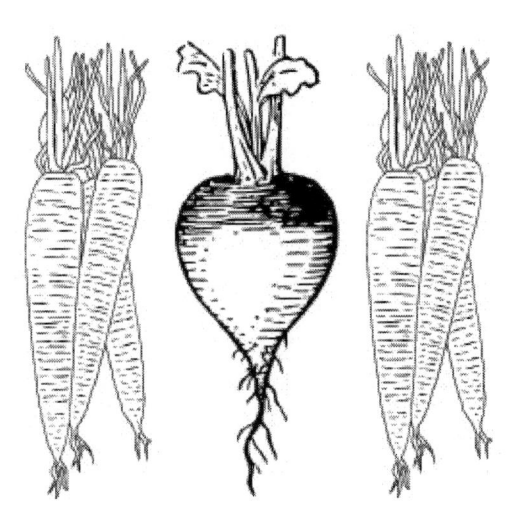

Mission 32: Banish that draught

A Green Superhero knows that a cold draught in your Superhero HQ is never a good thing.

A draught is an unwanted cold breeze that blow through your house – usually caused by gaps in windows and doors.

Draughts are bad because in the wintertime they let in too much cold air. This means that we need to use more energy (and money) to heat our homes.

Draught proofing is one of the cheapest and best ways to stop cold air coming in and save energy.

If you have a cold breeze coming from underneath one of your doors why not make your very own animal draught excluder – just search "Make your own draught excluder" online for great examples.

Why not ask whoever looks after you if they know that they could save money by draught proofing

Be a superhero: Draught-proof your home.

Mission 33: Buy Second-Hand

A Green Superhero knows that secondhand is super – except for plasters!

A true superhero knows that buying second-hand clothes is awesome because it saves money and the environment at the same time.

Did you know that a lot of water and chemicals go into making our clothes? Around 1,800 gallons of water are required to make one pair of blue jeans.

By buying second hand clothes, we are living a more sustainable life and saving lots of water in countries where our clothes are made but water is hard to find.

Buying second-hand clothes has never been easier. By going to online stores like EBay, you can buy lots of amazing used clothing. Alternatively, why not take a bag with you to your local charity shop and see what you can find.

Be a superhero: Buy second-hand clothes

COLOUR ME:

Mission 34: Build a Superhero Home

You already know that bugs and insects are great for our planet – so why not build them a supercool "bug hotel".

Many pollinators are solitary insects like butterflies, moths, labdybirds and bees. These creatures do not live in colonies and need to find warm, dry spaces to build their nest and hibernate over the cold winter.

As humans build on more and more natural space that these insects call home, they are increasingly struggling to find places to nest and hibernate

A bug hotel is a great place for all sorts of creepy-crawlies to make themselves a cosy home.

Bug hotels are easy to make out of materials you have at home. You can place a bug hotel in a quiet spot in your garden, balcony or local park. Search "make your own bug hotel" on the internet for great instructions. If you don't have the necessary materials, you can buy bug hotels made from recycled materials from garden centre's and online retailers.

Be a superhero: Build a bug hotel to give insects a new home.

COLOUR ME:

Mission 35: Plant trees as you search

Did you know a Green Superheroes best power is the ability to plant trees every time they search the internet?

But it's not just superheroes that can do this.

Did you know that there is a search engine called **"ECOSIA"** which works just like Google and plants trees when you use them to search the internet? So far, "Ecosia" has planted over 108 million trees around the world.

Just like Google Ecosia makes money from showing adverts when you search for things on the internet.

The difference is that they use this money to help plant trees and support environmental projects around the world to make the world a greener and better place.

Just by switching your search engine on your computer, you can be responsible for planting hundreds of trees every year.

To begin planting trees go to **www.ecosia.org** to switch your search engine on phones, tablets and computers. Make sure you ask permission of the device owner before switching.

Be a superhero: Switch to Ecosia and begin planting trees around the world.

NATURE LOG:
Record all the animals, birds and insects you see in a week:

Mission 36: Thank you fridge

We already know that running the tap longer than we need is bad. But no one likes drinking warm water.

Every time you run the tap waiting for the water to cool down you are wasting loads of precious water. Did you know that 10% of people around the world do not have access to clean drinking water?

The good news is that there are a few simple ways to stop wasting this water. The first way is to put a washing up bowl in the sink when you run the tap. The water you collect can be used to water plants in your house or garden.

The second way to save water is to fill up a jug of water straight from the tap (without wasting any water) and put this in the fridge and let this cool down.

Be a superhero: Don't waste water running the tap for cold water - use a jug or a bowl!

Mission 37: Recycle your electronics

We all know Superheroes love technology. Just look at Iron Man and Batman, packing loads of gadgets.

But you will never see a Green Superhero just throwing their gadgets in the bin. This is because electronics like TVs, laptops, toys etc. contain hundreds of substances, which can be toxic including; mercury, lead, arsenic, cadmium and lots more.

Did you know we generate around 40 tons of electronic waste every year – that is the same as throwing away 800 laptops every second!

Most of our electronic waste is sent to big landfills and incinerators where it is burnt releasing harmful toxins into the air that are bad for the environment and for people.

To stop this, there are some simple solutions. The first option is to donate or sell electronics that are still working – this way the items life is extended making the most of the materials that went into making it.

The second option is to recycle your electronics. If an item is broken this is the best option. By taking it to a recycling center (find your nearest online) they will be able to recycle lots of the parts and then safely dispose of the toxic elements that can't be recycled.

Be a superhero: Recycle your old technology.

Mission 38: Super flush

By now we all know that Green Superheroes try to save as much water as possible.

Did you know that you can save loads of water every time you flush the toilet with a simple Superhero hack? With the help of an adult fill up a plastic bottle with water. Lift the lid on the back of the toilet tank and gently place the filled water bottle into the tank.

Placing the bottle in the tank means that the tank will not fill up with as much water. This means that when you flush you will use less water.

Be a superhero: Reduce the flush of your toilet.

Mission 39: Green Fingered

No matter where a Green Superhero lives, they should always be surrounded by plants.

There are loads of different houseplants that you can grow very easily. Some can be used for soothing sore skin (aloe vera) while others can eat flies (Venus flytrap).

Having plants in your home has a whole bunch of benefits including: making your house look nicer, purifying the air in your home, improving mental health and lowering stress.

Most houseplants require very simple care giving them regular water and sunlight.

Be a superhero: Grow a houseplant

Mission 40: Plastic Free Picnics

Who doesn't love a picnic? You can't beat eating a tasty sandwich sitting on a picnic blanket in the sun.

The fastest way to ruin a great picnic though is to spoil it with loads of unnecessary plastic packaging, disposable plates and cutlery.

Did you know that over 40 billion plastic knives, forks and spoons are thrown away every year? Most plastic cutlery is too contaminated and small to be recycled meaning it goes straight into bin polluting our planet for hundreds of years to come.

The good news is that there are loads of super cool environmentally friendly alternatives. Instead of using disposable cutlery and plates why not, purchase a picnic set with plates, cups and cutlery that will last you a lifetime.

If you need disposable cutlery, plates and cups why not check out biodegradable bamboo alternatives, which can be bought online.

Instead of wrapping your sandwich in tinfoil, Clingfilm or a plastic sandwich bag, why not purchase a re-useable sandwich wrap that can be used over and over again.

Be a superhero: Find environmentally friendly alternatives to throw away picnics.

CHOOSE TO REUSE

By reusing you are:

Preventing pollution
Saving energy
Reducing Greenhouse Gases
Saving money
Reducing waste
Extend products life

Mission 41: Support Green Heroes

Did you know there are loads of awesome groups doing amazing work in your area that you could help?

All around the world, including near you there are charities and groups helping to make the world a better place. Whether it's a local group keeping your streets and fields clean of rubbish, a charity providing shelter for animals or activists fighting to stop climate change there is something for everyone.

Why not search online to find a cause you would be interested in helping. You could offer support by donating some pocket money or volunteering some time to help.

Can't find a group working on an issue you care about? Why not start your own group and get your friends involved. It is amazing what we can do when we all come together.

Be a superhero: Support a charity by donating pocket money or volunteering.

Mission 42: Tree-mendous 2

Trees are secret superheroes. Their superhero power is the oxygen they create for us to breathe.

Simply without trees, humans would not exist. We rely on them for the air we breathe every single day but they are also super important for tackling climate change, droughts and floods.

However, across the world trees are being cut down – every minute about 36-football pitches worth of trees are lost to deforestation.

This is why it is so important that we look after the trees in our gardens, woods and forests.

As a Green Superhero, it is our job to try to protect our natural environment as best we can.

Planting new trees is a great way to protect the environment, create a natural habitat for birds and insects and help cool the climate.

You can help by getting your hands messy and planting a tree at home either in the garden or on a balcony if available. Alternatively you can sponsor the planting of a tree by simply typing, "Sponsor a tree" into your internet search engine.

Be a superhero: Plant a tree.

Mission 43: Fossil Fuel Free Day

It is amazing how much energy we use every day without thinking about it.

Turning on the lights, cooking our dinner, watching TV or riding in a car. They all use up energy warming up the planet.

So that you can understand how much energy you use in a day why not try to do a fossil fuel free day. To do this don't use any energy from when you wake up until you go to bed.

This means no turning on the lights, not using any electricity, not using the oven to cook or car to drive and no phones, TVs or laptop.

Why not turn it into an adventure and have an indoor camp using candles and torches for light. By the end of the day, you will see just how much energy you would normally use in a day.

Be a superhero: Complete the fossil fuel free day challenge.

Mission 44: Upcycling

Upcycling – no it's not riding a bicycle upside down. That really would be superhero stuff.

Upcycling is taking something that is old, broken or you no longer want and transforming it into something new and awesome.

There are loads of great examples on the internet of upcycling projects you could do. How about transforming your old welly boots into a plant pot. This way your old wellies won't go in the bin and you don't have to buy a new plant pot. By upcycling goods, you can extend their life, save money and the environment.

Be a superhero: Have a go at an upcycling project.

Mission 45: Re-Useable

The Coronavirus can seem scary. But by taking simple steps, you can protect yourself, others and the planet.

We already know what we need to do to stop Coronavirus spreading – wash our hands, wear a mask, socially distance and isolate if we show signs of being poorly.

But did you know that it is estimated that 194 billion disposable masks and gloves are being used and thrown away each month. That's loads of extra plastic waste polluting our planet.

What makes it even worse is that a lot of these masks and gloves are being littered rather than put in a bin.

This is causing lots of harm to birds and animals who trapped in the elastic of masks or suffocating on gloves.

There is a simple solution to help reduce the impact of necessary protective equipment. If you can, always choose a reusable mask that you can wash. This reduces the amount of waste you create.

If you need to use disposable masks to protect wildlife always, cut off the elastic before throwing them away.

Be a superhero: Use a re-usable mask. Always cut the elastic on disposable masks if you have to wear one.

WILD ADVENTURES:

Tick the adventures off as you complete them.

CLIMB A BIG HILL	
GO ON A SCAVENGER HUNT	
GO STAR GAZING	
BUILD A DEN IN THE WOODS	
CAMP OUTDOORS	
WATCH A SUNRISE AND SUNSET IN THE SAME DAY	
MAKE SOMETHING COOL OUT OF NATURE	
GO GEOCACHING	
MAKE AND SAIL TWIG RAFTS	

Mission 46: Old-School

Did you know that there is a superhero who brings you milk while you sleep?

Their name - The Milkman. Milkmen have been delivering glass bottles of milk to people's doors for years.

Glass bottles are amazing; because once you have used them they can be collected, washed and used again and again meaning no waste. The milkfloats used to deliver the milk are also amazing as they are 100% electric – and often charged from renewable sources.

This all means you can have milk delivered to your house while you sleep and help the environment.

Be a superhero: Switch your plastic milk bottles for glass bottle delivery.

Mission 47: Buy Ethical

While we try our best to reduce, reuse and recycle we have to buy things like food, clothes and other necessary items.

Because we don't want to hurt our planet, it is important that when we buy new things we try to find the most ethical options possible.

One simple way to look for the most ethical options is to look for trusted labels such as:

- Organic (by the Soil Association)
- Vegan (by the Vegan Society)
- Fairtrade (by the Fairtrade Foundation)
- FSC Recycled (by the Forestry Stewardship Council)

By looking for trusted labels, we know that we are buying the best options possible to reduce the impact on our planet, wildlife and people involved in making our goods.

Be a superhero: Buy ethical choices that are good for people, wildlife and planet.

WORDSEARCH

R	A	I	N	F	O	R	E	S	T
R	G	I	M	N	C	Z	C	O	R
V	F	B	O	K	E	P	U	I	E
E	R	Y	H	J	A	J	T	L	E
R	E	V	A	W	N	S	A	D	S
S	M	O	U	N	T	A	I	N	R

| OCEAN | RAINFOREST | RIVERS |
| SOIL | MOUNTAIN | TREES |

Mission 48: The 3Ps

Toilets are smelly superheroes. They are a clean way for us to get rid of all our smelly pee and poo.

The problem is that people flush all sorts of things down the toilet, which is bad news for our sewers and our environment.

That is why the only thing should be flushed away are the 3Ps – **PEE, POO and TOILET PAPER.**

When we flush anything other than the 3Ps down the toilet, we can create blockages in the sewers that take our toilet waste away. These blockages can cause sewers to flood spreading poo and pee into our rivers.

Be a superhero: Only flush the 3Ps

Mission 49: Speak Up

If we want to see action taken on issues like climate change, we need to make some serious noise….

In the UK, every town has an MP – someone elected to represent that area in Parliament.

Your MP is responsible for tackling issues in your town and raising concerns to Government on behalf of people like you.

So, Why not have a think about a problem you would like your MP to tackle maybe plastic pollution, climate change or animal welfare and send them an email asking them to take action.

Be a superhero: Write to your MP.

Mission 50: Share this book

Hopefully if you have got this far you have enjoyed this book and have completed all the missions.

By completing the missions in this book, you have learnt how to be a Green Superhero.

There is now just one mission left for you to complete – share this book!

By sharing this book with someone else, you are re-using the book, making the most of the paper, and encouraging someone else to become a Green Superhero. Soon you will have your own superhero squad.

Be a superhero: Share this book and build your own Green Superhero Gang.

A GREEN planet IS A CLEAN PLANET

Awesome Resources

Below are some awesome places to check out if you are looking for more information:

www.natgeokids.com

www.wwf.org.uk

www.theclimatecoalition.org

www.climatekids.nasa.gov

www.nationaltrust.org.uk/50-things-to-do

www.sas.or.uk

www.uk.buymeonce.com

www.tearfund.org

www.waterwise.org.uk

www.rspb.org.uk

www.ethicalconsumer.org

Printed in Great Britain
by Amazon